SWEET TOMATOES

Written by Barbara Botch
Illustrated by Lisa J. Michaels

Sweet Tomatoes

by Barbara Botch

ISBN: 9781939288264
Library of Congress Control Number: 2013947973

© 2013 by Barbara Botch

Illustrated by Lisa J. Michaels

Published in the U.S.A.

This is a work of fiction. Names, characters, places and incidents are the product of the author's and the illustrators imagination or are used fictitiously.

All rights reserved.
Published by Poet's Crossing, an imprint of Wyatt-MacKenzie, Inc.

No part of this publication may be reproduced or used in any form without the prior written permission of the author, illustrator and publisher.

For more information please write to:
poetscrossing@wyattmackenzie.com

This book is dedicated to Oliver Raymond Botch and Joseph Michael Botch, my two grandsons, who taught me that love continues to find us and each time it is sweeter than the time before.

If a child takes joy from the love of his family
and honors the poetry in his heart,
then there is nothing to keep
the lad's life from becoming
a beautiful work of art.
Barbara Botch

A special thank you to my brother Tim Brozovich
for his genuine interest over the years in whatever I was working on.
I will miss him forever.

Also by Barbara Botch

Poet's Crossing

Poems by Barbara Botch

TOMATO PLANTS

Tomato plants are growing
in our garden one – two – three.
One for Daddy, Mommy too,
and there's also one for me.

MEATBALL

Meatball is my puppy's name.
He's big and brown, and cool.
He waits at home and sleeps all day
while I'm away at school.

PANCAKES

Pancakes are my favorite food for breakfast with my mom. Daddy likes to make the eggs while Grandma sings a song.

JOJO B.

My baby brother is so cute.

We call him JoJo B.

I love him more than anything.

Oh boy, how he loves me!

SINGING IN THE SUNSHINE

I'm happy and I'm smiling.

My eyes are twinkling too.

I've eaten all my breakfast,

deciding what to do.

A stroller ride sounds lovely.

We can sing our favorite song.

We'll drink in lots of sunshine

as our Meatball tags along.

BASEBALL

Standing on the home base
waiting for the ball,
my bat wiggles back and forth,
aiming for the wall.

It's one swing - two swings -
three swings and then...
my coach brings the tee up and
the ball flies on the wind!

Papa is watching.
There's pride on his face.
The ball's in the outfield as
I sprint past first base!

CRAWLING

I'm crawling now from here to there,
on my hands and knees, you'll see.

Daddy holds a toy out front
and I crawl to it with ease.

I pick it up and smile real big,
back on my bum I sit.

Mommy gets the camera
while I just rest a bit.

LEARNING TO WHISTLE

You blow out.
I blow in.
A whistle comes
and we do it again.

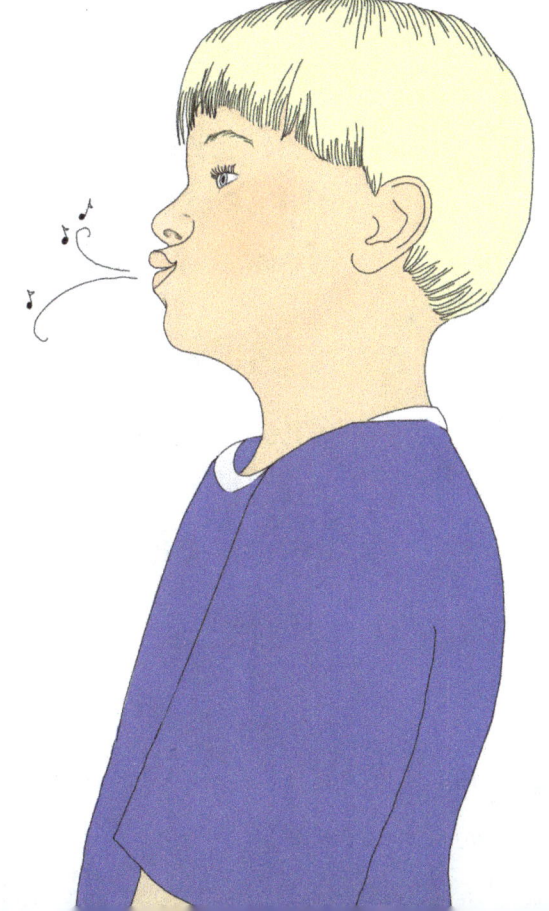

HOW TO TRAP A LEPRECHAUN

Trapping a Leprechaun
isn't all that hard,
if you dig a deep hole
in your own backyard.

You won't lure him with gold,
he's got quite enough.
So don't even try it,
he'll just call your bluff.

Just leave him two pieces
of chocolate cake,
three sugar-plum pies
or four strawberry shakes.

He'll fall asleep fast
and when he awakes,
he'll have a surprise
and a big tummy ache!

MY GRANDMA AND ME

My Grandma came down.
We went to the sea.
We searched for seashells,
my Grandma and me.

She brought a blanket.
I came with a toy.
Softly she whispered,
"I love you my boy."

"Let's share these cookies,"
she said with a smile.
"And when we're all done,
we'll walk for a while."

I reached for her hand.
Our hearts were set free.
We danced down the beach,
my Grandma and me.

KILLARNEY TOWN

Oh, Grandma's going to take me
to Killarney town one day.
She said when I am grown a bit
that we'll be on our way.

She said I'll love the rolling hills,
the music that they sing.
I'll wear my little Irish hat and
buy the Claddagh ring.

Now she told me about my daddy
that when he was only twelve,
they took the plane together
in search of Irish elves.

They got a car and drove around
they even kissed the stone but
there's nothing oh nothing oh nothing she says
as the likes of Killarney Town.

Oh! there's nothing oh nothing oh nothing
like the lovely Killarney Town.

So I'm going to close my eyes now
and dream a dream of you.
I'll think about the leprechauns
It's all that I can do.

So Grandma I'll wait patiently
until I hear you say,
I've grown a bit,
let's pack our clothes
for we are on our way!

CUBS GAME

My uncle is a Cubs fan.
He took me to a game.
We rode the train to L.A.
and watched the Cubbies play.

We each had a hot dog,
cotton candy too.
We watched and cheered with every hit
for the guys in red and blue.

It was getting late as night games do.
The score was four to three.
We only needed two more runs
but I'd have to wait and see.

Back on the train I fell asleep
and dreamed about the game.
"Would they do what they had to do
to bring the team to fame?"

Next morning I woke
to my uncle's voice,
"Do you want
to know the score?"

"Yes! I do!
Did we win?"
"Cubbies five
the Dodgers four."

MY OWN MAILBOX

I have my own mailbox that sits near the door.
I love to get letters, cards and much more.
I've gotten such things as coloring books,
some sticker pages too.
I love how my family knows what I like,
giving me lots of fun things to do.

PAPA'S DOG, MURPHY

He came to visit the other day
and he stayed with us while Pop was away.

I could not sleep a wink with him here.
He stretched all night and he cuddled too near.

He panted and panted all night long.
He licked, he whined and his breath was too strong.

I went to preschool the very next day,
exhausted from Murphy's night time horseplay.

I grumpily waited. Nap time came around.
I drifted to sleep without making a sound.

When Mommy arrived, I grabbed my backpack
and then we went home to have a nice snack.

Next to me, Murphy waited for a crumb.
I said, "Let's have a talk," and I gave him one.

"I'm glad that you're here, but if I had known,
last night I would have been sleeping alone!"

"Tonight will be different," I said with a smile.
"You'll just have to snore on the floor for a while."

That night he drooled with his feet in the air,
and I slept much better, without any dog hair.

MAC AND CHEESE

Mommy and Daddy try hard every day
to feed me all the right stuff.

It's not always easy to convince me.
Sometimes it is really tough.

I'd rather eat Mommy's cookies
and often a fuss I make.

On days like today, when I had to eat peas
before having birthday cake.

They tell me it's very important
to eat healthy every day.

To get bigger, stronger and have energy
when friends ask me out to play.

"Okay, I believe! I'll do as you say
if I can have one thing that I like."

"Please," I ask, "Can I have some mac and cheese
before I go ride on my bike?"

AH - CHOO

I'm sneezing and coughing
and blowing my nose,
staying in bed with lots
of warm clothes.

Drinking lots of water,
my face is all red,
Mommy keeps kissing me
on the forehead.

I'm not very happy.
JoJo gets to play
while I lay down,
staying out of his way.

Daddy goes to work and
gets home around four.
I'm happy when I hear him
come through the door.

He lets me get up and
we watch some baseball,
then back to my bed,
with tissues I sprawl.

The next morning comes and
I'm feeling just fine.
The sun is shining,
it's already nine.

I go to the kitchen.
Mom's making me toast.
Oh no! My brother
is blowing his nose.

TRICK OR TREAT

The gardeners are cutting down a tree.
A postman delivers mail.
Candy wrappers across the lawn
get picked up and put into a pail.

The witches and pumpkins
have all gone to sleep.
Oh so tired
after trick or treat.

A GIG WITH A JIG

They pulled out the pots
and all the pans too.

They woke up that morning,
knowing just what to do.

Their mom and their dad
jumped out of the bed,
Mommy just stood there,
her hands on her head.

"This is our band!" Oliver said.
"Me and JoJo now have a gig."

They all laughed with joy
as they listened and watched.

Meatball was doing a jig.

GLAD THERE IS YOU

Always say "Thank you"
at night in your prayers
for trees
and the flowers
and the love we have shared.

For without the trees
there would be no shade
to lay
on a blanket
slurping Mom's lemonade.

Without the flowers
there'd be no honey
for bee's
to collect on
the days that are sunny.

And without our love
just where would we be?
Lonely...
me without you
and you without me.

www.ingramcontent.com/pod-product-compliance
Lightning Source LLC
Chambersburg PA
CBHW081026040426
42444CB00014B/3371